EASY PIANO

TOP WORSHIP SONGS

ISBN 978-1-61780-558-5

HAL•LEONARD®
CORPORATION
7777 W. BLUEMOUND RD. P.O. BOX 13819 MILWAUKEE, WI 53213

Visit Hal Leonard Online at
www.halleonard.com

EVERLASTING GOD

Words and Music by BRENTON BROWN
and KEN RILEY

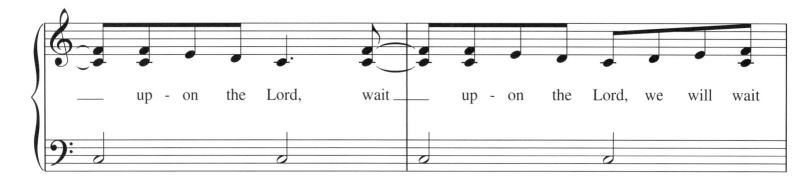

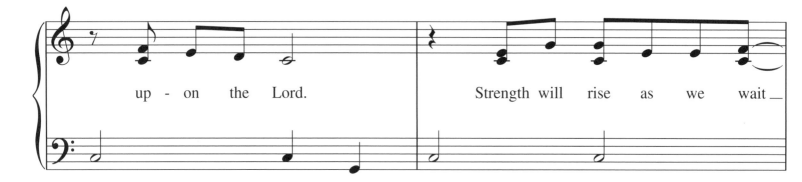

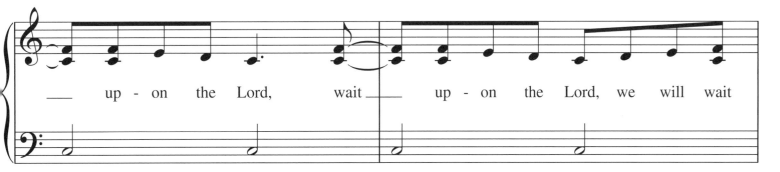

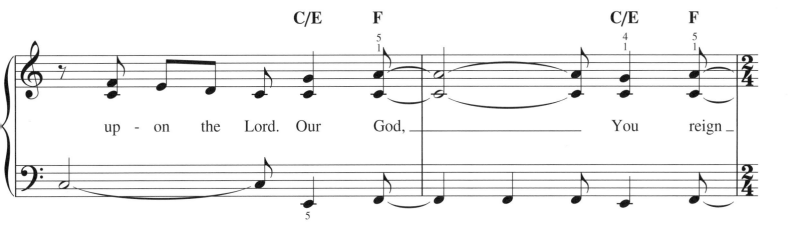

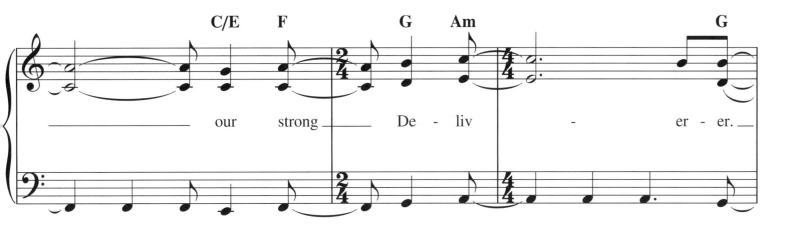

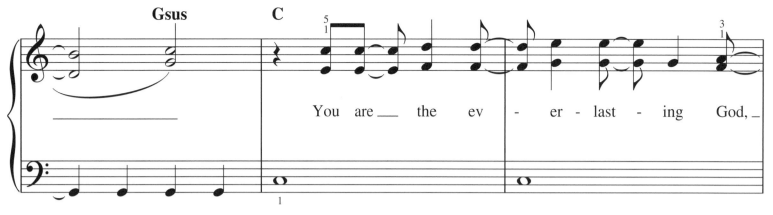

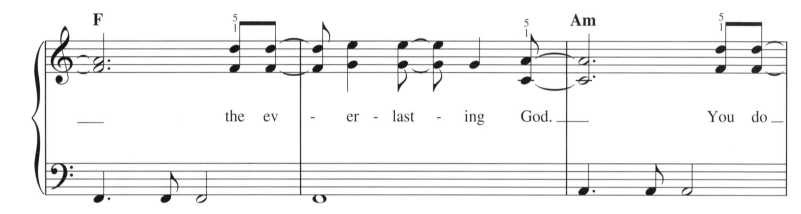

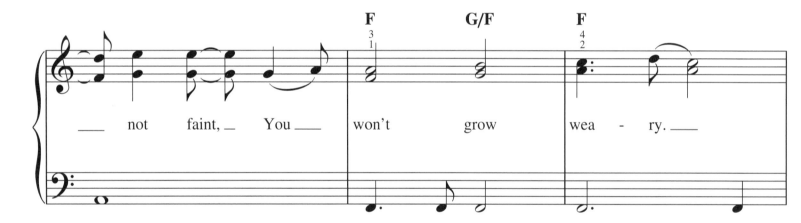

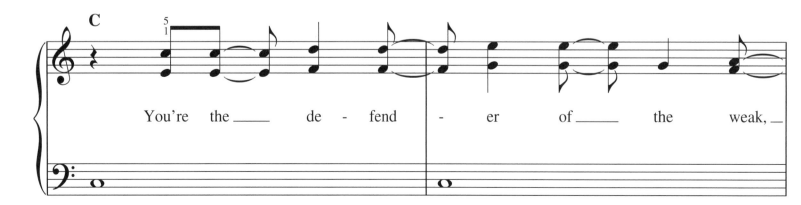

You com - fort those ___ in need, ___

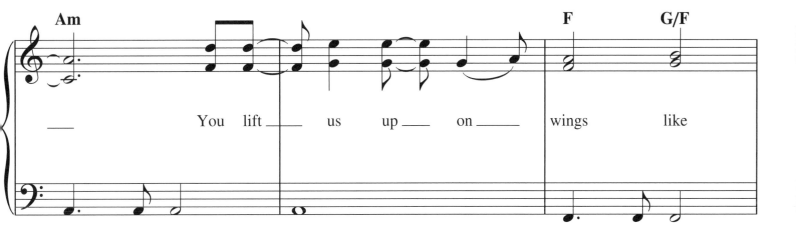

You lift ___ us up ___ on ___ wings like

ea - gles. ___   ea - gles. ___

FROM THE INSIDE OUT

Words and Music by
JOEL HOUSTON

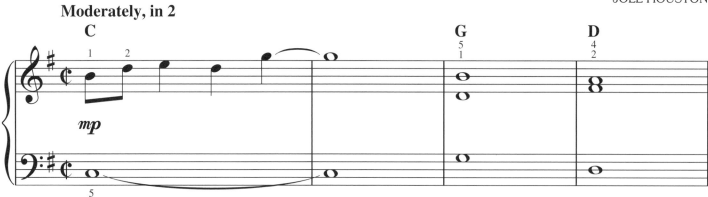

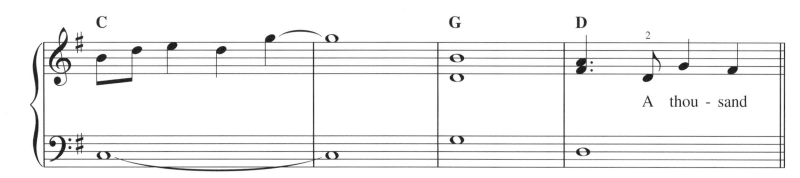

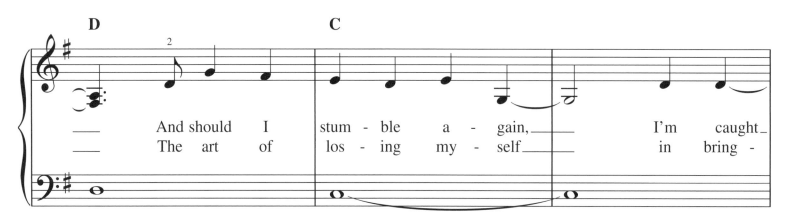

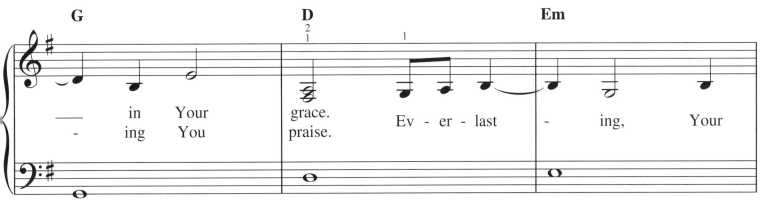

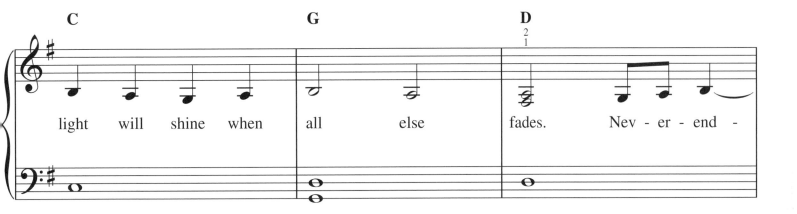

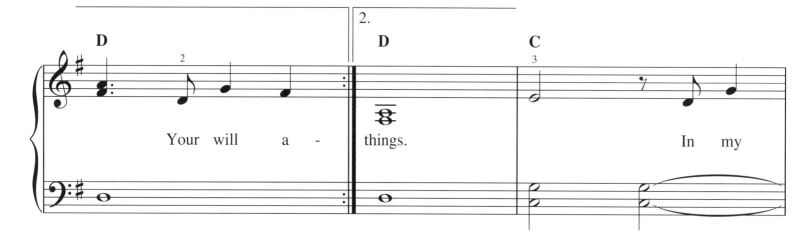

Your will a - things.   In my

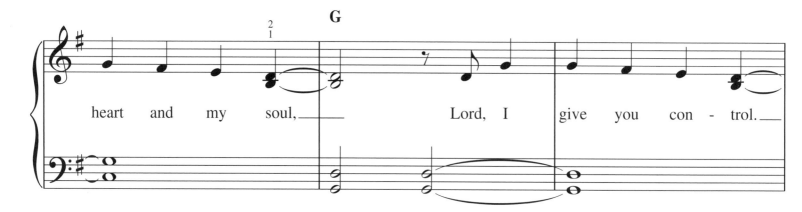

heart and my soul,____   Lord, I   give you con - trol.____

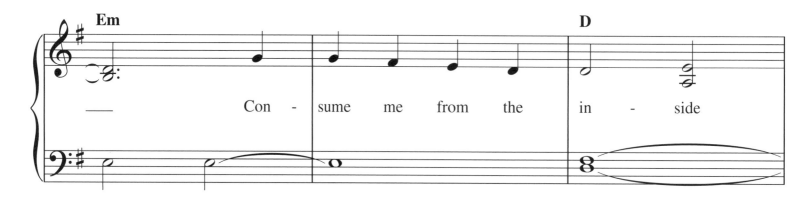

____   Con - sume me from the in - side

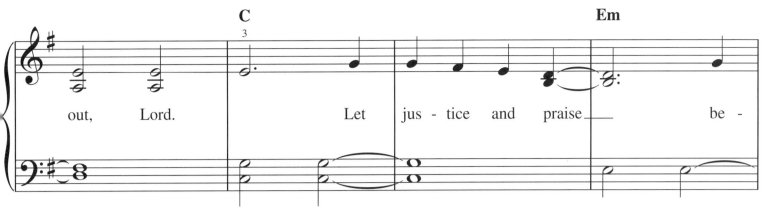

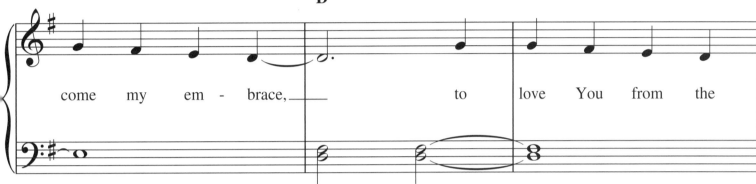

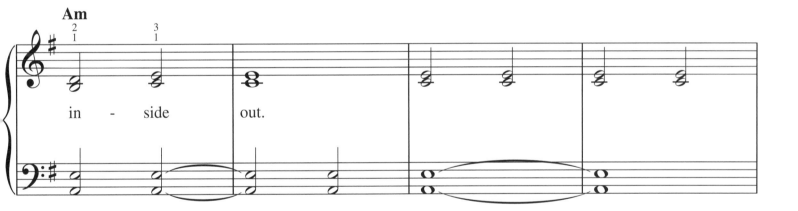

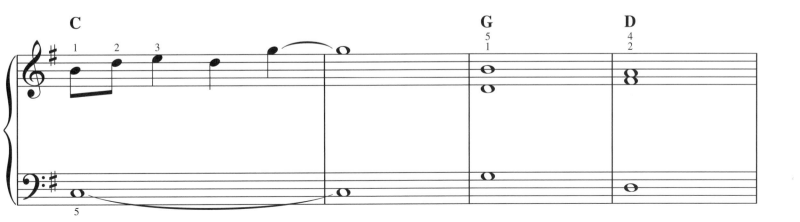

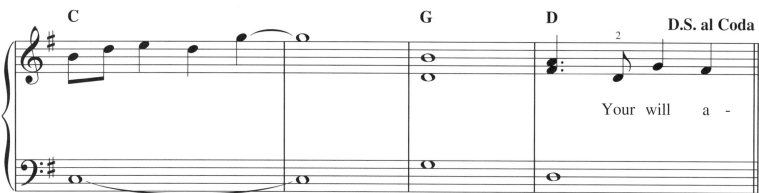

Your will a -

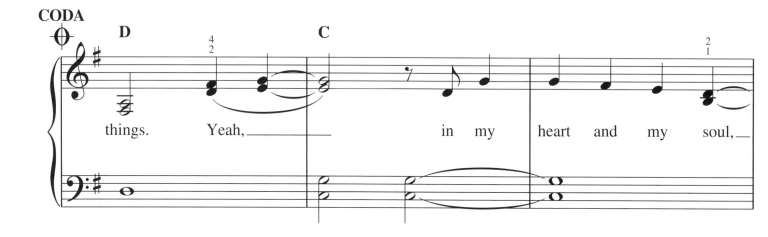

things. Yeah,___ ___ in my heart and my soul,__

Lord, I give you con - trol.___ ___ Con -

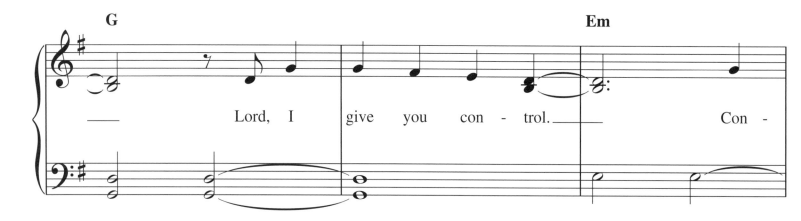

sume me from the in - side out, Lord.

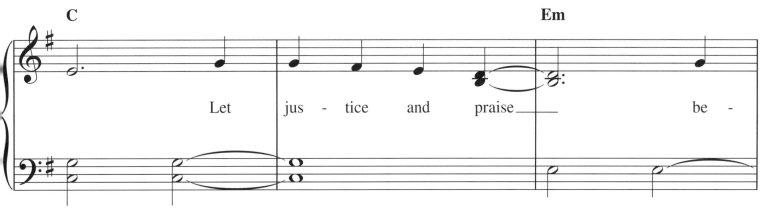

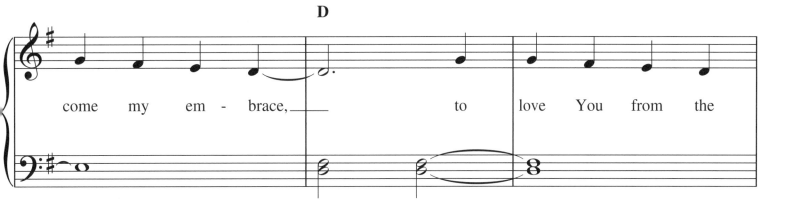

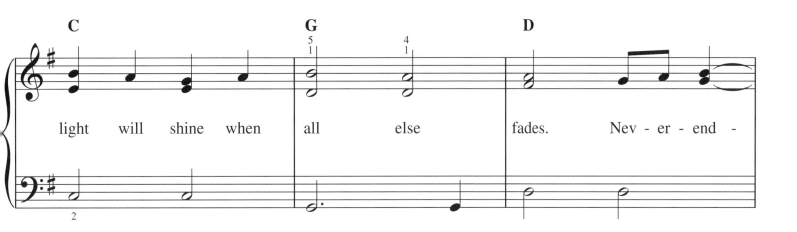

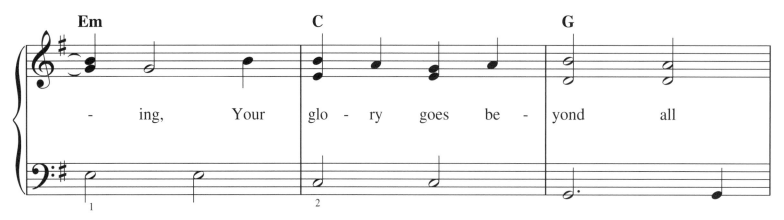

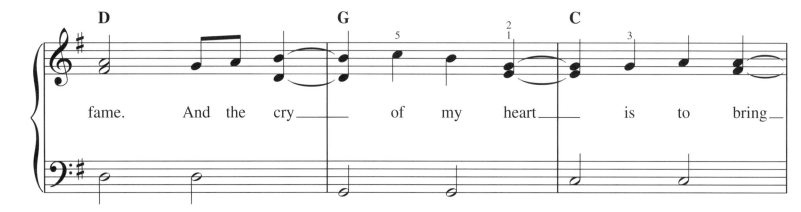

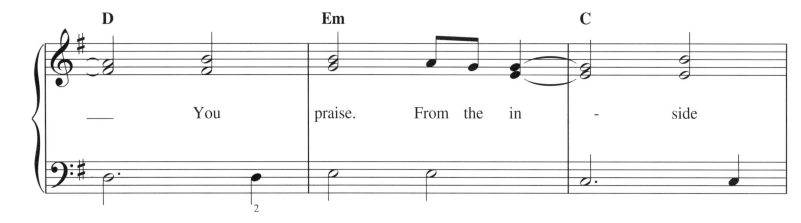

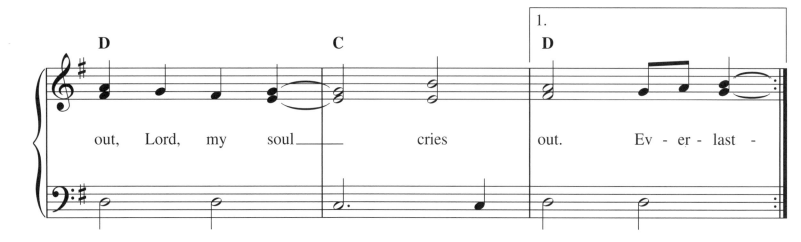

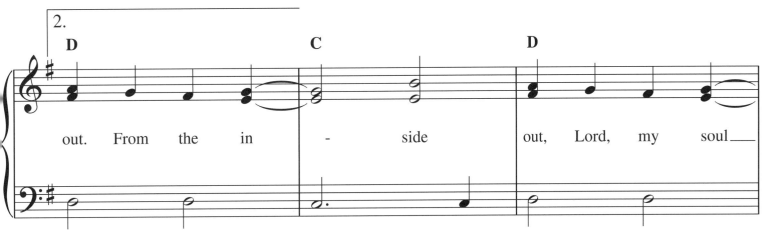

out. From the in - side out, Lord, my soul___

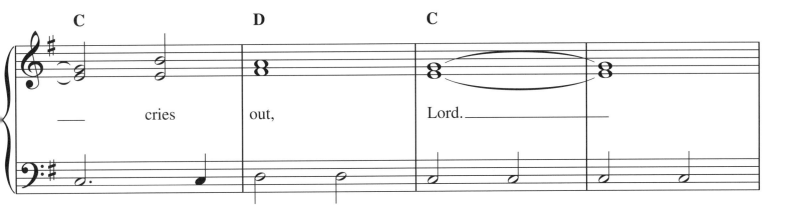

___ cries out, Lord._____

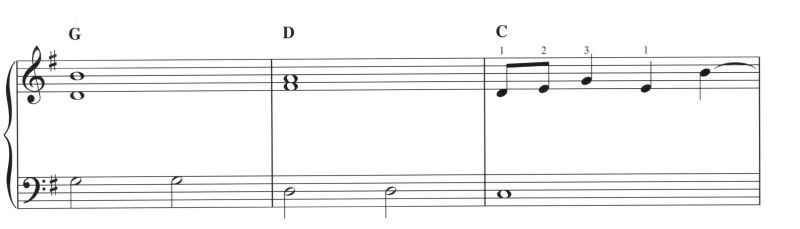

rit.

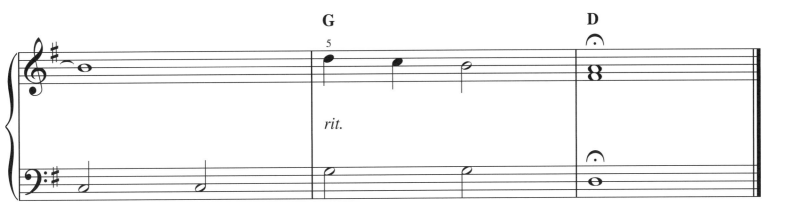

GLORY TO GOD FOREVER

Words and Music by STEVE FEE
and VICKY BEECHING

Moderate Rock

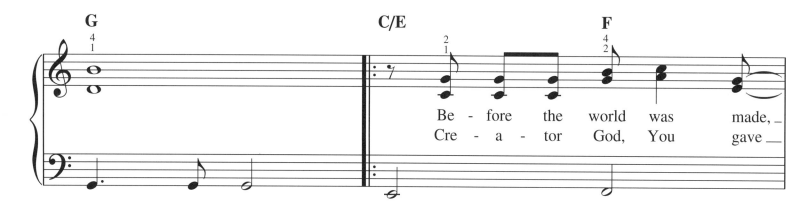

Be - fore the world was made,_
Cre - a - tor God, You gave __

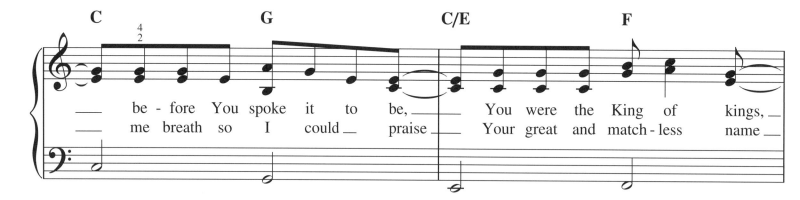

__ be - fore You spoke it to be,_ You were the King of kings,_
__ me breath so I could _ be, praise _ Your great and match - less name __

__ yeah, You were,_ yeah, You were. _ And now You're reign - ing still,_
__ all my days,_ all my days. _ So let my whole life be __

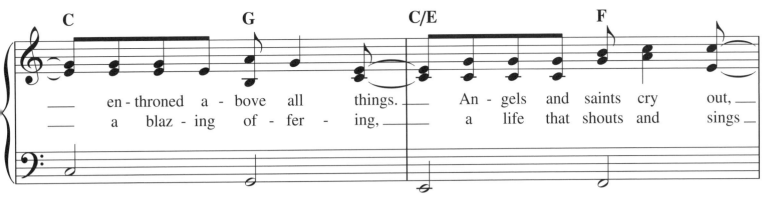

en - throned a - bove all things. ___ An - gels and saints cry out, ___
a blaz - ing of - fer - ing, ___ a life that shouts and sings __

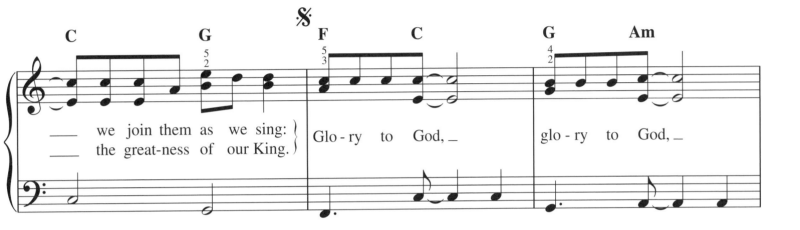

___ we join them as we sing: Glo - ry to God, _ glo - ry to God, _
___ the great-ness of our King.

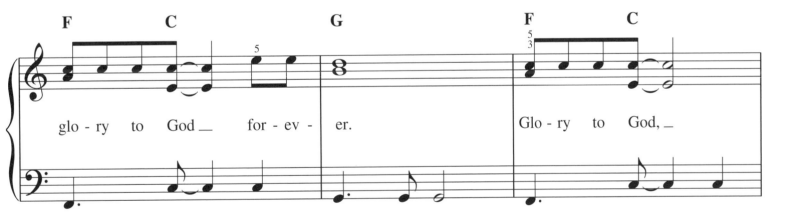

glo - ry to God _ for - ev - er. Glo - ry to God, _

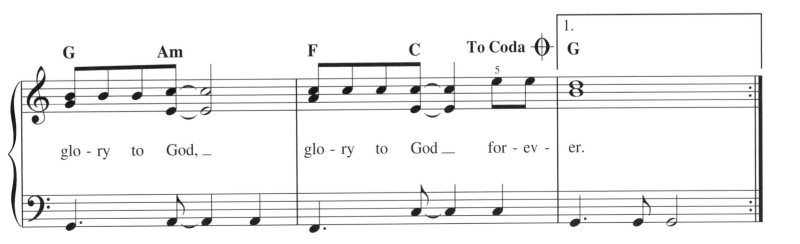

glo - ry to God, _ glo - ry to God _ for - ev - er.

OFFERING

Words and Music by
PAUL BALOCHE

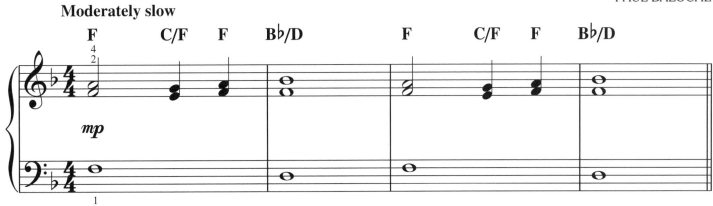

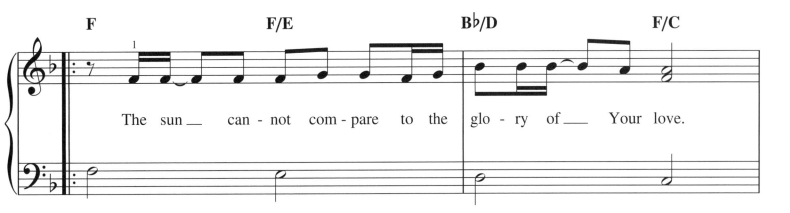

The sun __ can - not com - pare to the glo - ry of __ Your love.

There is __ no shad - ow in Your pres - ence.

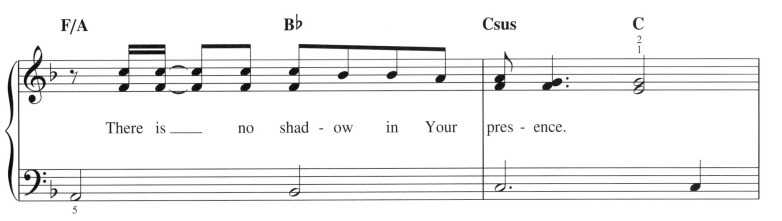

No mor - tal man would dare to stand be - fore __ Your throne,

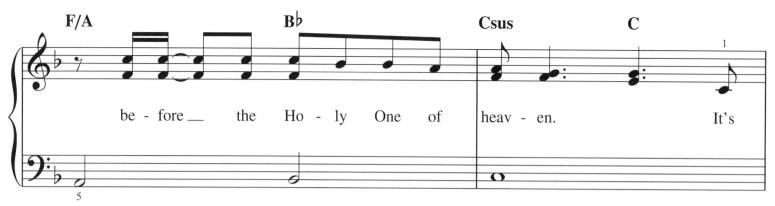

be - fore ___ the Ho - ly One of heav - en. It's

on - ly by ___ Your blood and it's on - ly through ___ Your mer - cy,

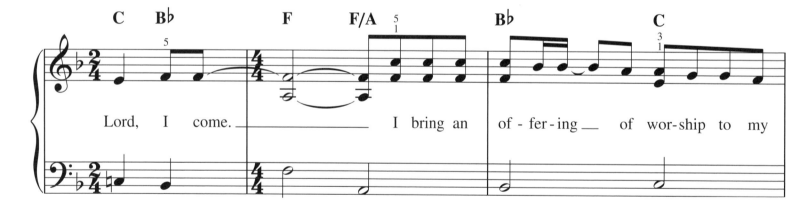

Lord, I come. ___ I bring an of - fer - ing ___ of wor-ship to my

King. ___ No one on earth de - serves ___ the prais - es that I

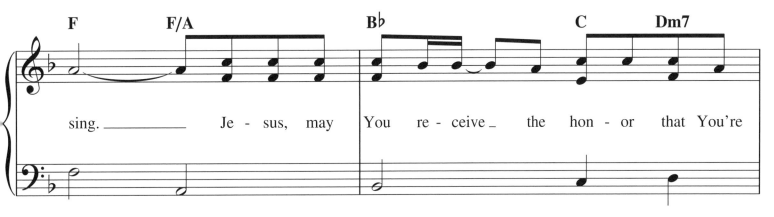

sing. _____ Je - sus, may You re - ceive _ the hon - or that You're

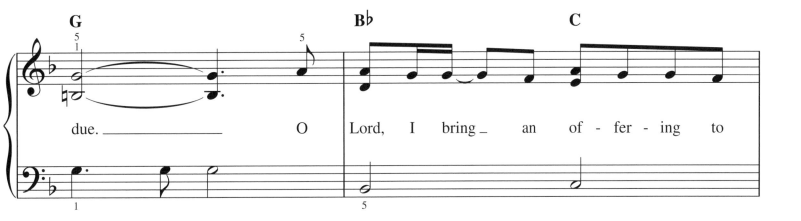

due. _____ O Lord, I bring _ an of - fer - ing to

You.   I bring an of - fer - ing to

You.   You.

HOSANNA

Words and Music by
BROOKE FRASER

the whole earth shakes.

I see His love and mer - cy

wash-ing o - ver all our sin; ___ the peo - ple sing, ___ the peo - ple sing. ___

___ Ho - san - na, ___ ho - san - na, ___ ho -

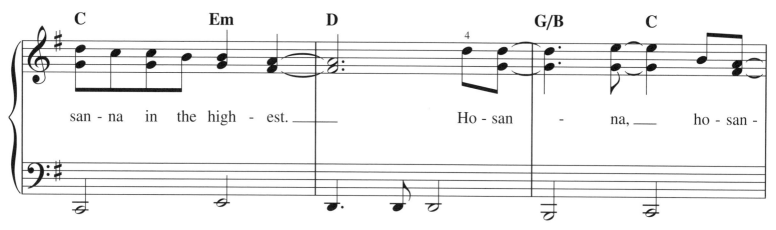

san - na in the high - est. ___ Ho - san - na, ___ ho - san -

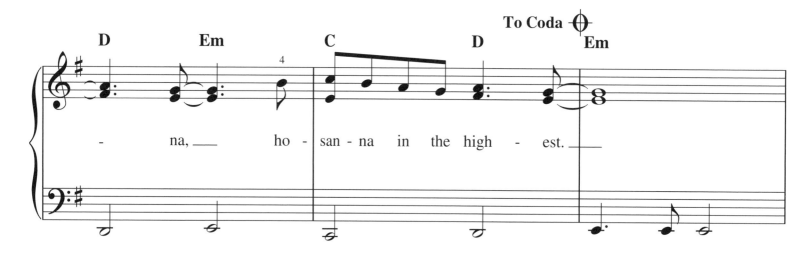

- na, ___ ho - san - na in the high - est. ___

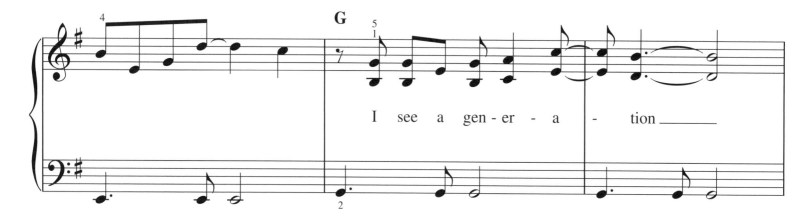

I see a gen - er - a - tion _____

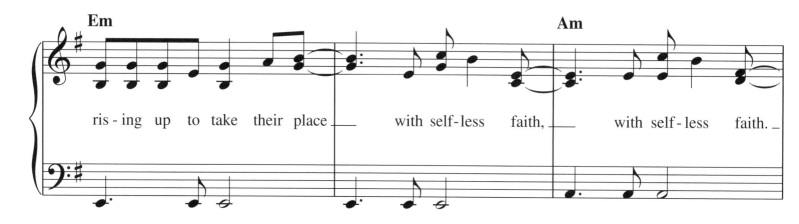

ris - ing up to take their place ___ with self-less faith, ___ with self-less faith. ___

I see a near re - viv - al

stir-ring as we pray and sing; we're on our knees, we're on our knees.

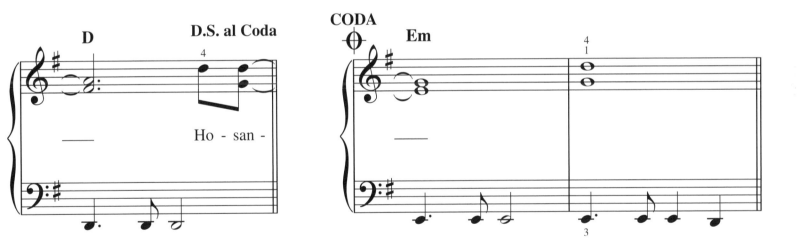

D.S. al Coda

Ho - san -

CODA

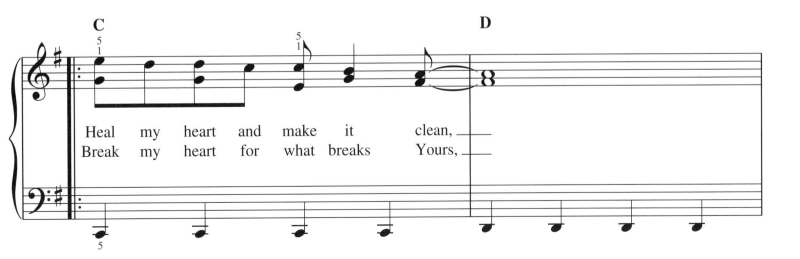

Heal my heart and make it clean,
Break my heart for what breaks Yours,

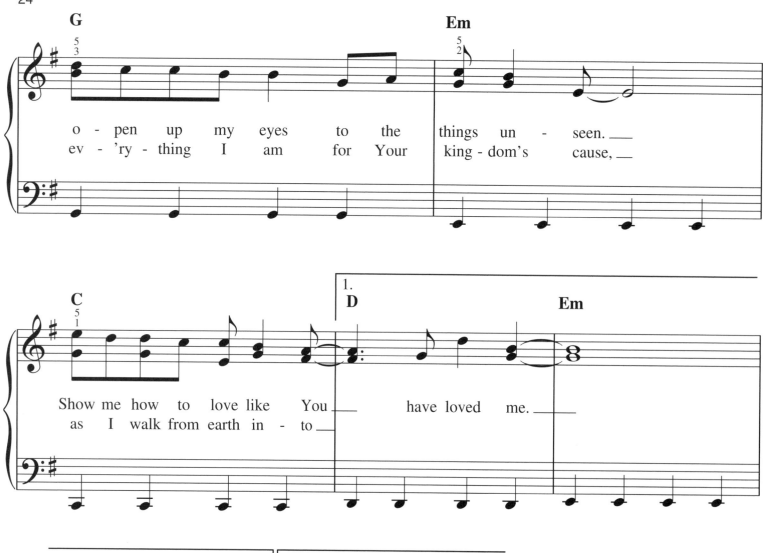

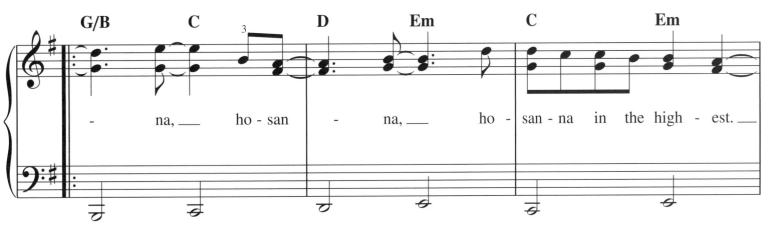

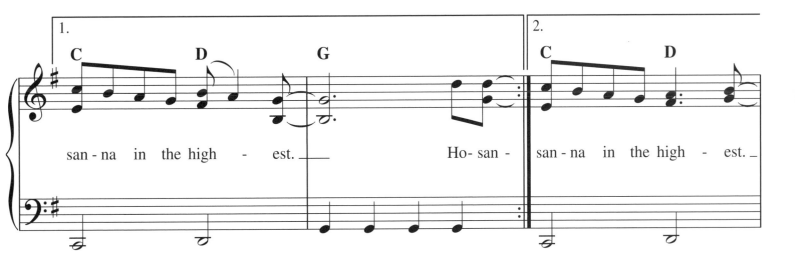

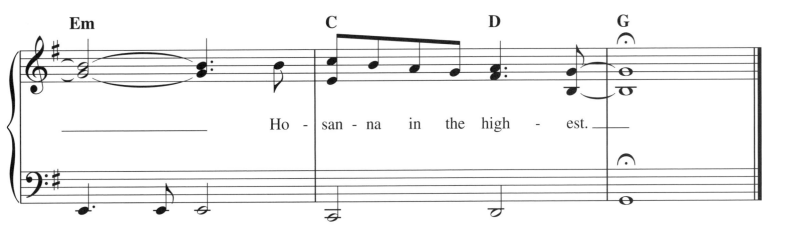

HOW HE LOVES

Words and Music by
JOHN MARK McMILLAN

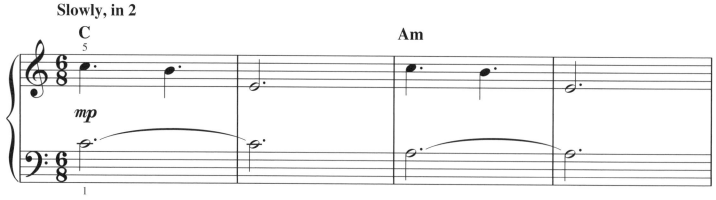

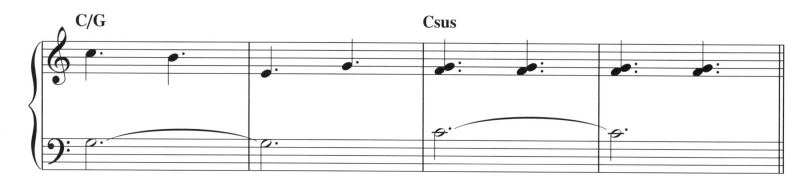

He is jeal-ous for me. Loves like a hur-ri-cane; I am a tree,

bend-ing be-neath the weight of His wind and mer-cy. And

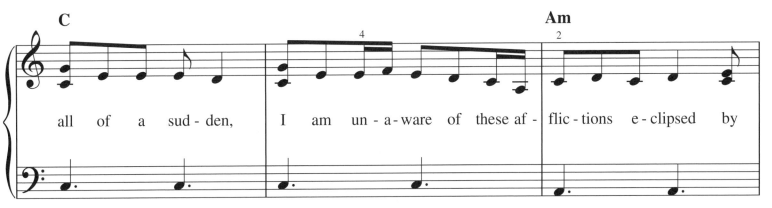

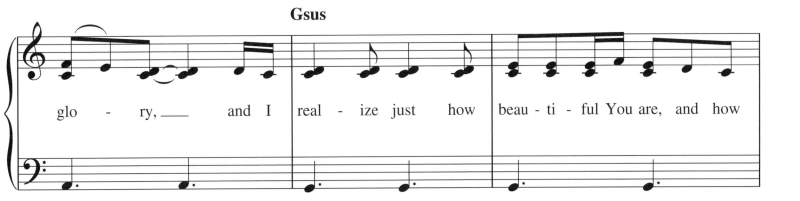

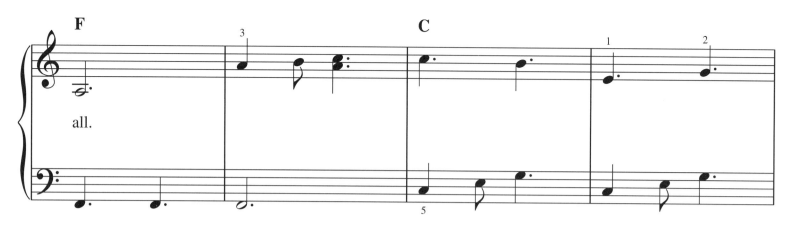

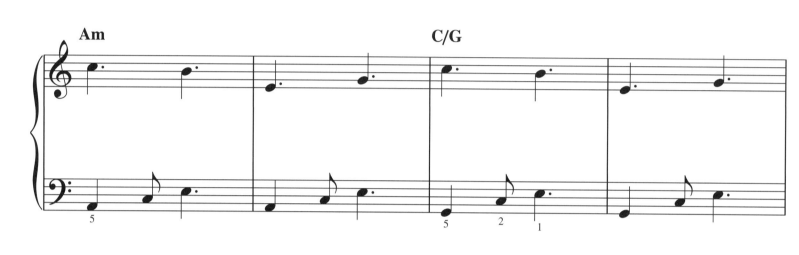

Yeah, He loves us.

Oh, _____ how He loves us. Oh, _____ how He loves us.

Oh, ___ how He loves. ___ And we are His por - tion and

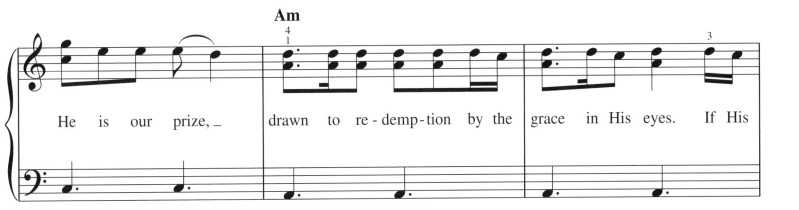

He is our prize, _ drawn to re - demp - tion by the grace in His eyes. If His

grace is an o - cean, we're all sink - ing. ___ And

heav - en meets earth like an un - fore - seen kiss, and my heart turns vio - lent - ly in-

Yeah, He

loves us. Oh, _____ how He loves us. Oh, _____ how He

loves us. Oh, _____ how He loves.

I AM FREE

Words and Music by
JON EGAN

will praise, __

through You __ the dark - ness flees, __

through You __ my heart __ screams, "I am free! __

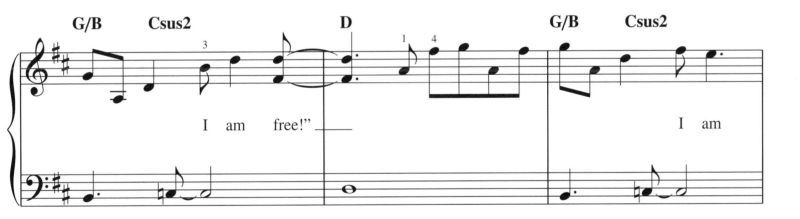

I am free!" __

I am

free to run. __

(I am free to run.) __

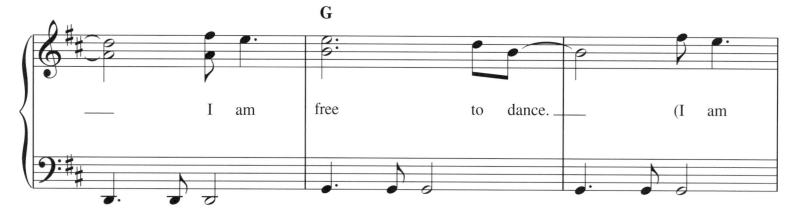

I am free to dance. ___ (I am

free to dance.) ___ I am free to live ___ for You. ___

___ (I am free to live ___ for You.) ___ I am free. ___

___ (I am free.) ___ I am free. ___ (I am free.) ___

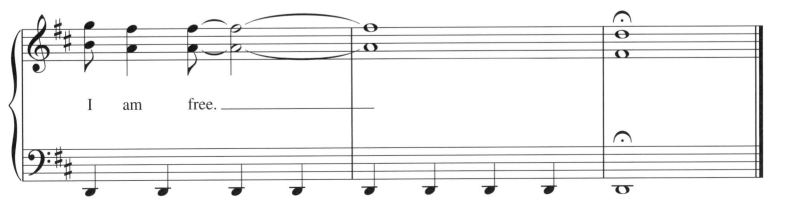

I WILL RISE

Words and Music by CHRIS TOMLIN, JESSE REEVES,
LOUIE GIGLIO and MATT MAHER

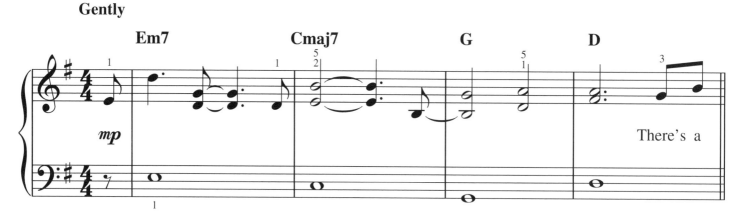

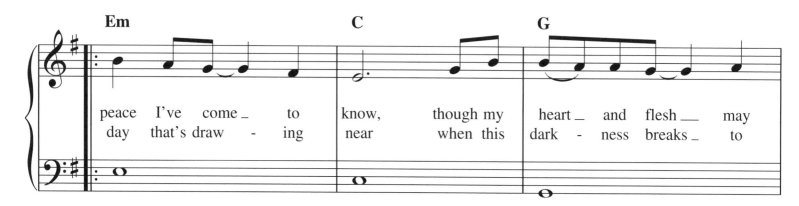

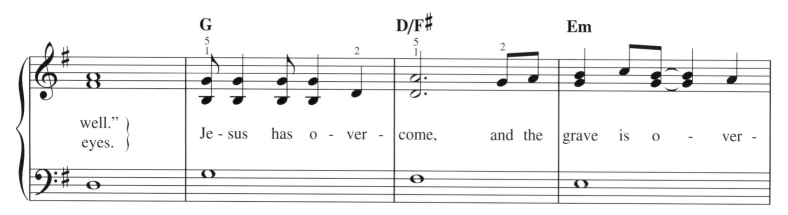

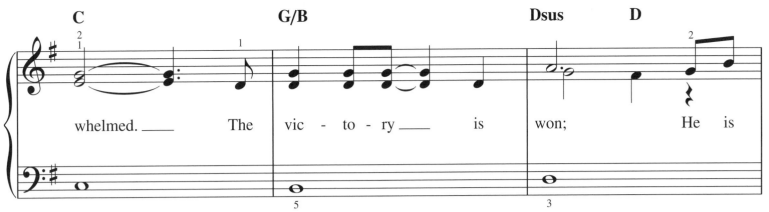

whelmed. _____ The vic - to - ry _____ is won; He is

ris - en from _ the dead. And I _____ will rise _____ when He calls _

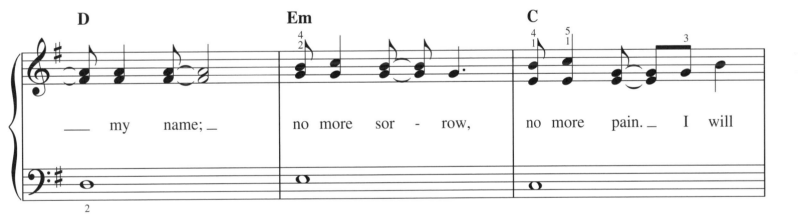

_ my name; _ no more sor - row, no more pain. _ I will

rise on ea - gles' wings; _ be - fore my God _ fall

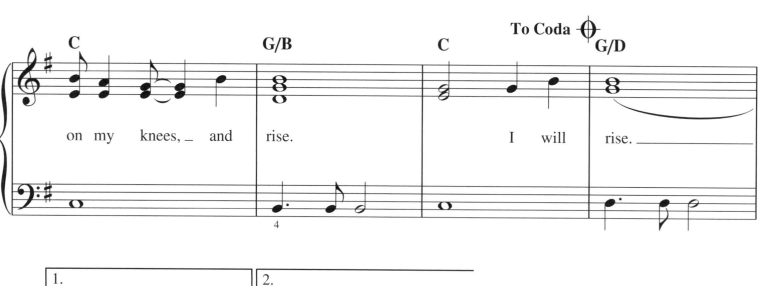

on my knees, _ and rise. I will rise. _____

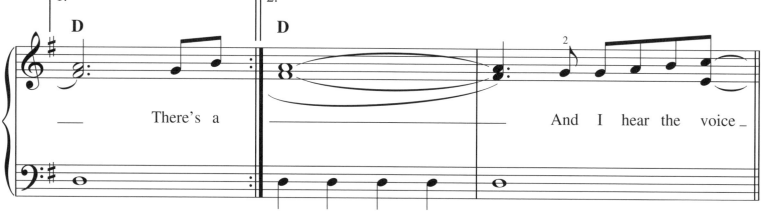

1. ___ There's a   2. _____ And I hear the voice _

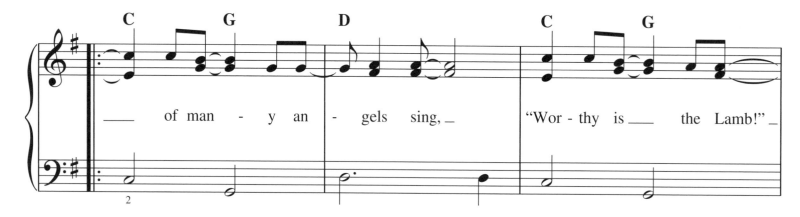

___ of man - y an - gels sing, _ "Wor - thy is ___ the Lamb!" _

___ And I hear the cry ___ of ev - 'ry long - ing heart, _

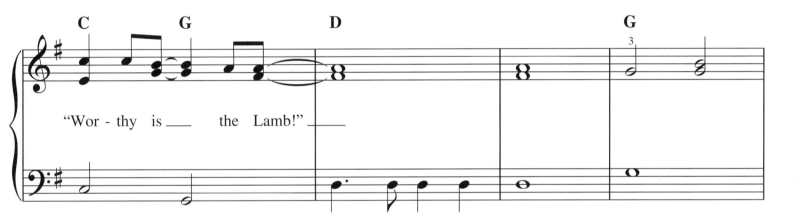

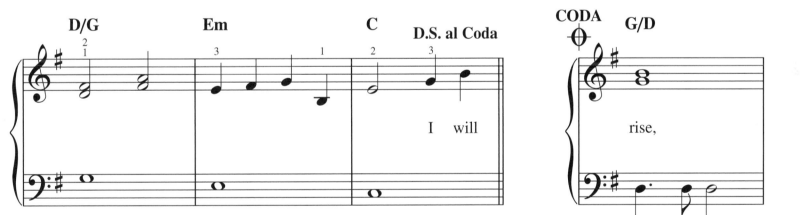

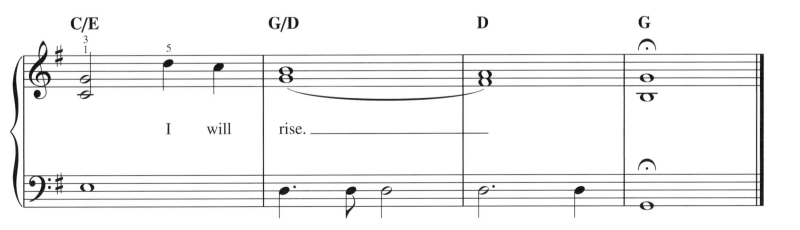

MY SAVIOR LIVES

Words and Music by JON EGAN
and GLENN PACKIAM

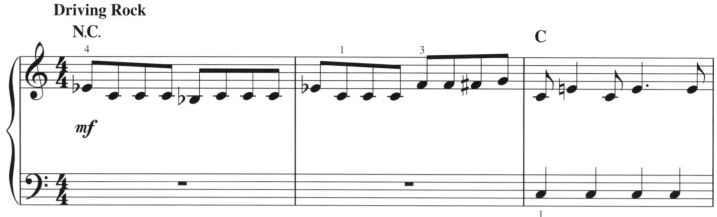

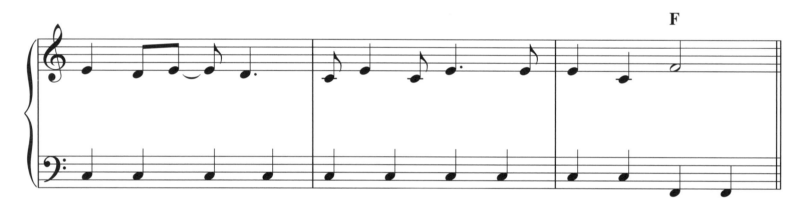

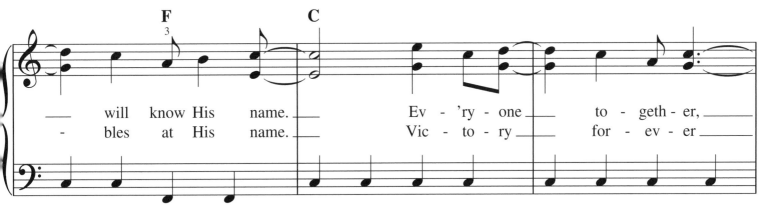

will know His name. Ev - 'ry - one to - geth - er,
- bles at His name. Vic - to - ry for - ev - er

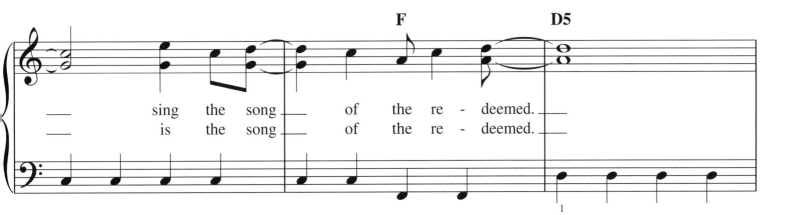

sing the song of the re - deemed.
is the song of the re - deemed.

I know that my Re - deem - er lives,

and now I stand on what He did. My Sav - ior,

42

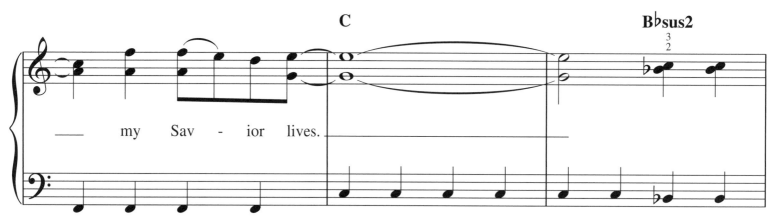

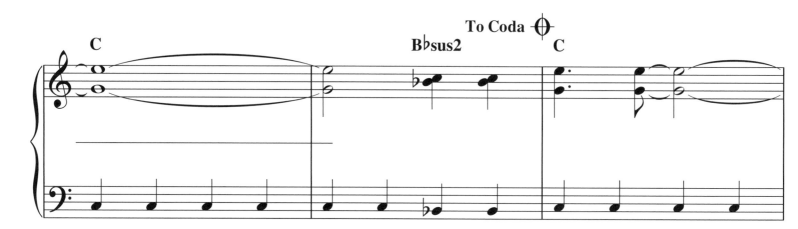

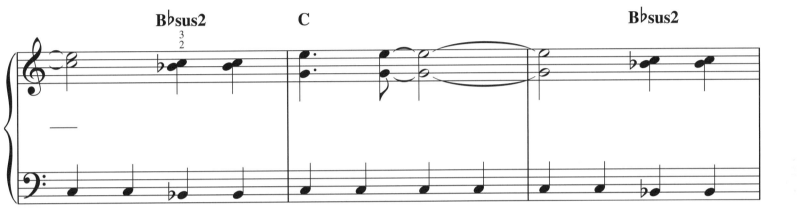

44

lives.   mf   My

Sav - ior _____ lives.   My   Sav - ior _____

lives.   My   Sav - ior _____ lives.

D.S. al Coda

CODA

I   know that my ___   Re - deem- er   lives, _

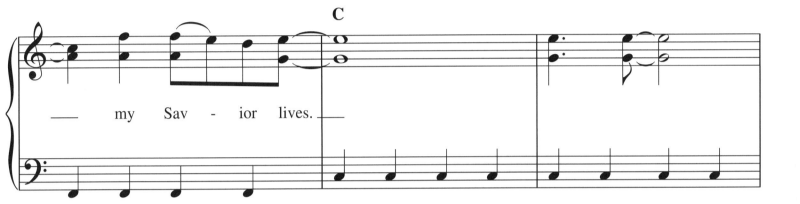

THE STAND

Words and Music by
JOEL HOUSTON

You stood be - fore ___ cre - a - tion, ___ e -

ter - ni - ty in ___ Your hands. ___ And You spoke the earth ___ in - to mo -

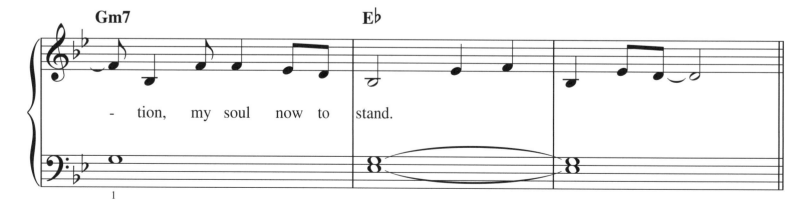

- tion, my soul now to stand.

You stood be - fore _____ my fail - ure, _____ and
I walk up - on _____ sal - va - tion, _____ Your

car - ried the cross _____ for my shame. _____ My
Spir - it a - live _____ in me. _____ This

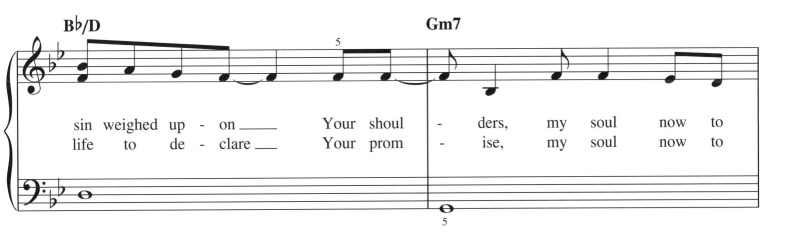

sin weighed up - on _____ Your shoul - ders, my soul now to
life to de - clare _____ Your prom - ise, my soul now to

stand.
stand.
So what could I _____ say? _____

48

What could I ____ do, ____

but of - fer this heart, ____ O God, ____ com - plete - ly to

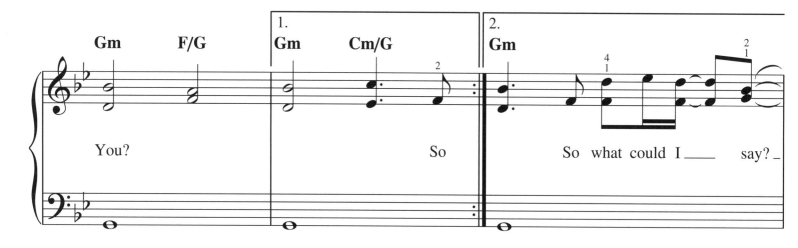

You? So So what could I ____ say? ____

And what could I ____ do, ____

but of-fer this heart, __ O God, __ com-plete-ly to

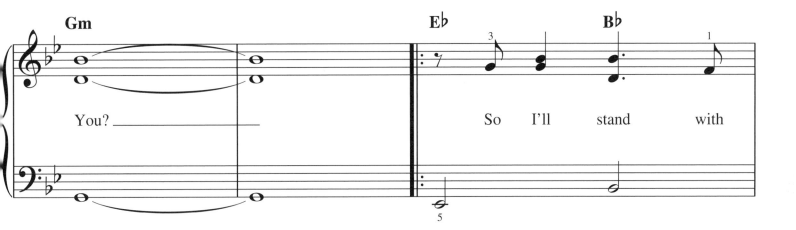

You? _____ So I'll stand with

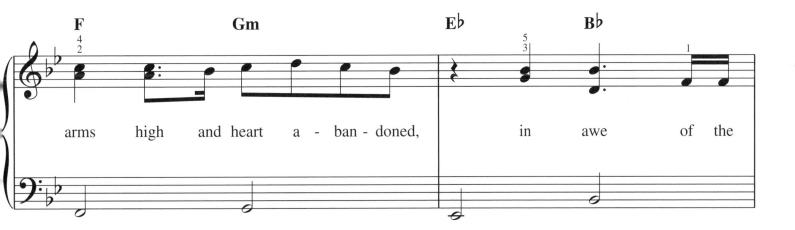

arms high and heart a - ban - doned, in awe of the

One who gave it all. __ I'll stand, my soul, Lord, to You sur - ren - dered.

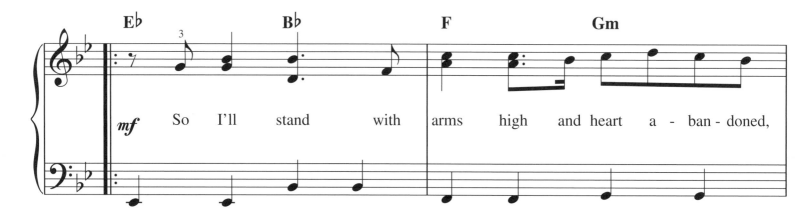

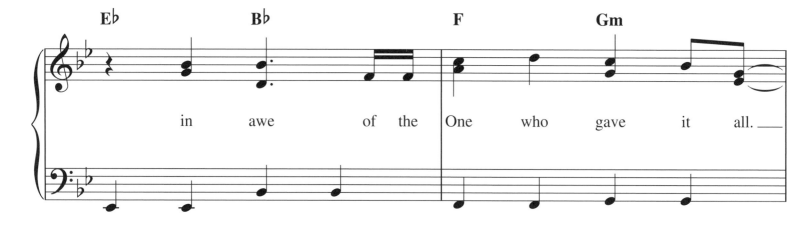

All I am ___ is Yours. ___

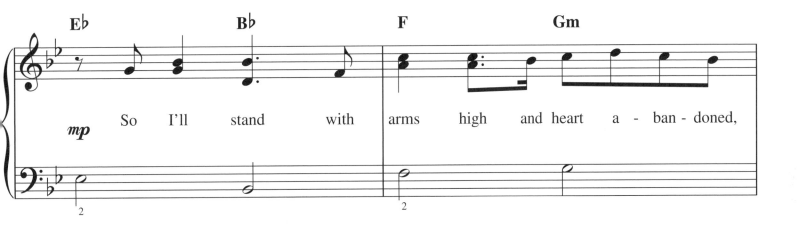

mp So I'll stand with arms high and heart a - ban - doned,

in awe of the One who gave it all. ___ I'll stand, my

soul, Lord, to You sur - ren - dered. All I am ___ is Yours. ___

TODAY IS THE DAY

Words and Music by LINCOLN BREWSTER
and PAUL BALOCHE

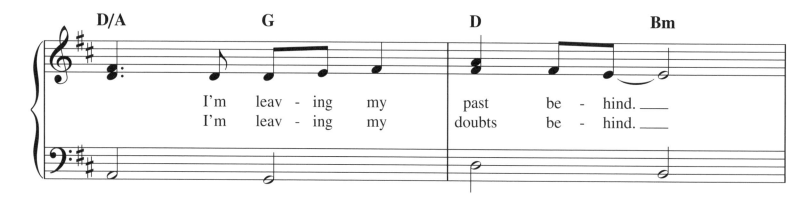

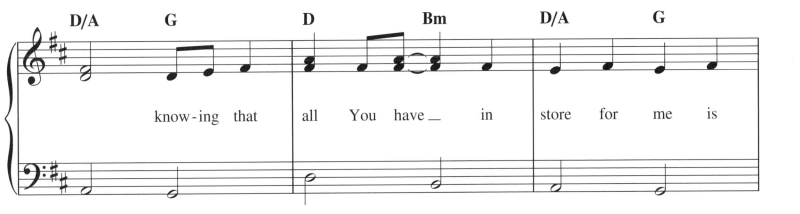

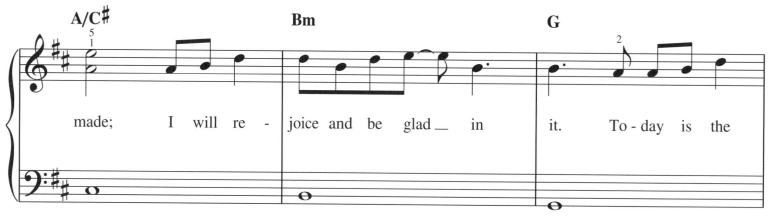

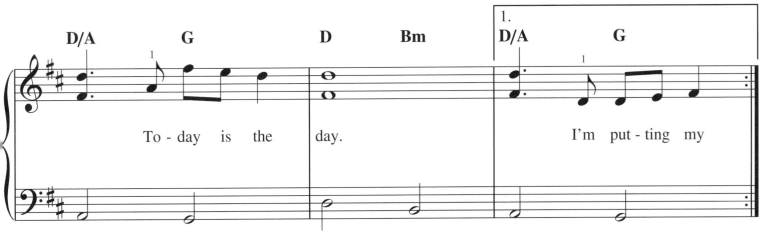

To - day is the day. I'm put - ting my

I ____ will stand ___ up - on ___ Your truth. ___ (I ___

____ will stand ___ up - on ___ Your truth.) ___ And all ___ my days ___ I'll live ___

____ for You. ___ (All ___ my days ___ I'll live ___ for You.) ___ I ___

2.

D · G

_____ my days _____ I'll live. To - day is the

D · A/C# · Bm

day You ___ have made; I will re - joice and be glad ___ in

G · D · A/C#

it. To - day is the day You ___ have made; I will re -

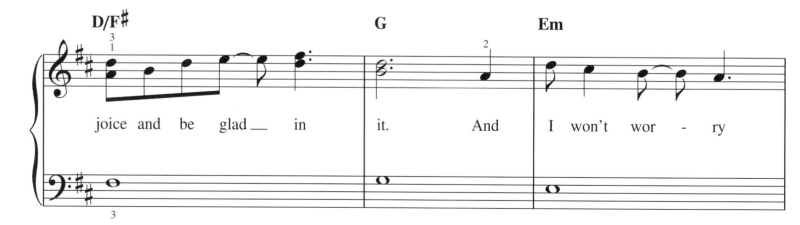

D/F# · G · Em

joice and be glad ___ in it. And I won't wor - ry

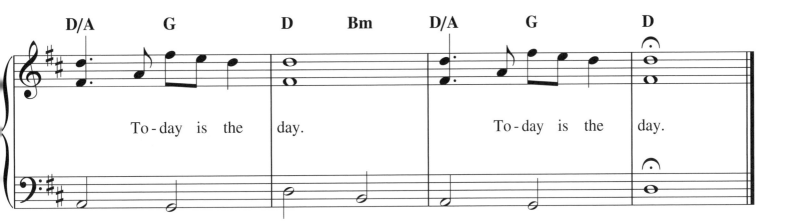

REVELATION SONG

Words and Music by
JENNIE LEE RIDDLE

Moderately slow

Wor - thy is the Lamb who was slain.

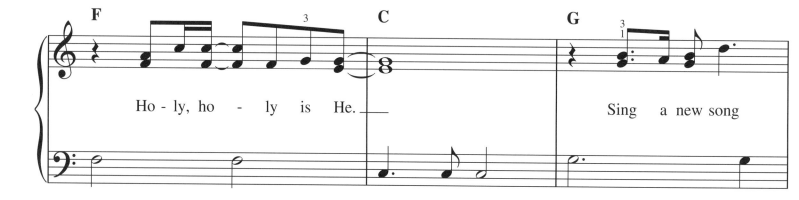

Ho - ly, ho - ly is He. Sing a new song

to Him who sits on Heav-en's mer-cy seat.

Ho - ly, ho - ly, ho - ly is the __ Lord God Al-might - y,

who was __ and is and is __ to come.

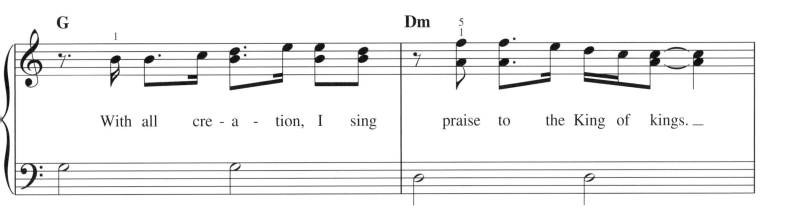

With all cre - a - tion, I sing praise to the King of kings. __

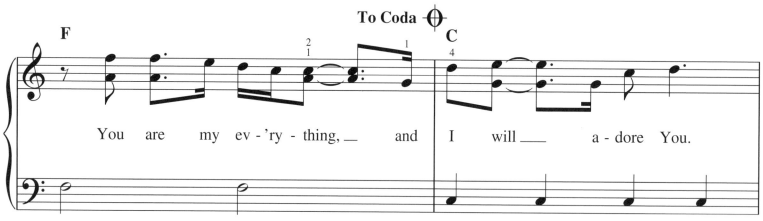

See begin

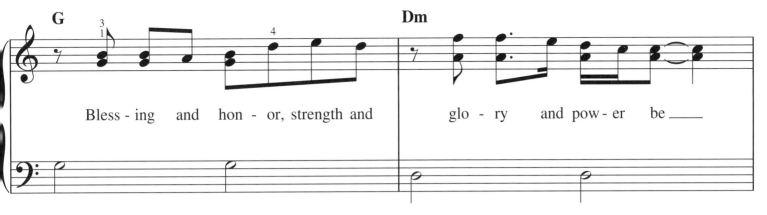

Bless - ing and hon - or, strength and glo - ry and pow - er be ___

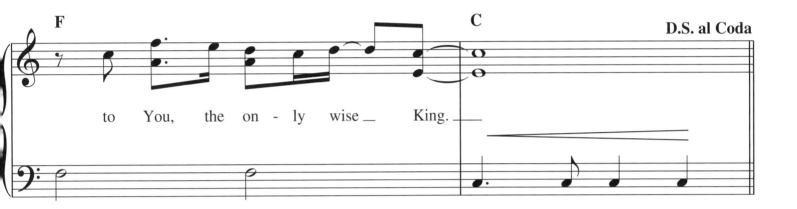

to You, the on - ly wise ___ King. ___

D.S. al Coda

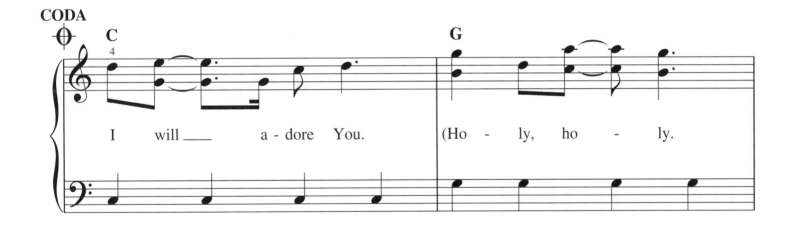

CODA

I will ___ a - dore You. (Ho - ly, ho - ly.

You are ho - ly.)

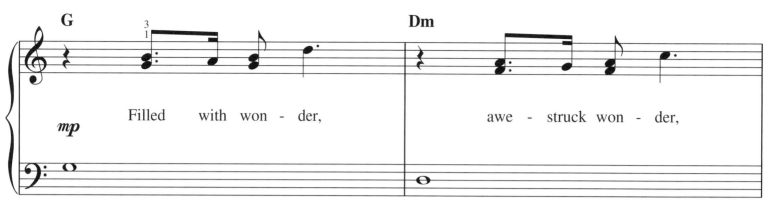

Filled with won - der, awe - struck won - der,

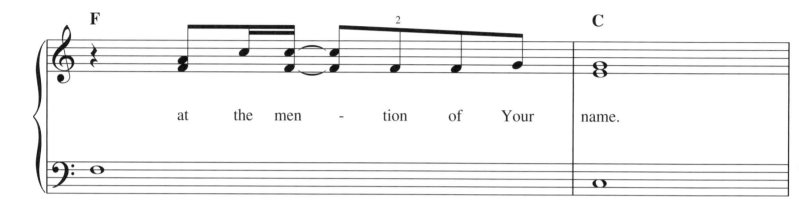

at the men - tion of Your name.

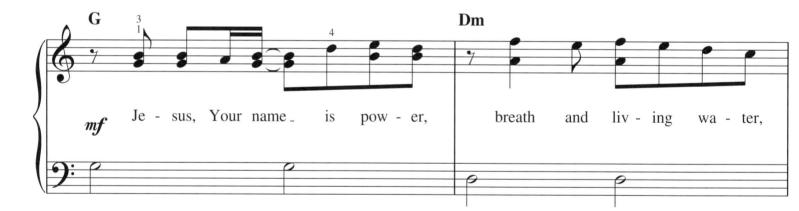

Je - sus, Your name is pow - er, breath and liv - ing wa - ter,

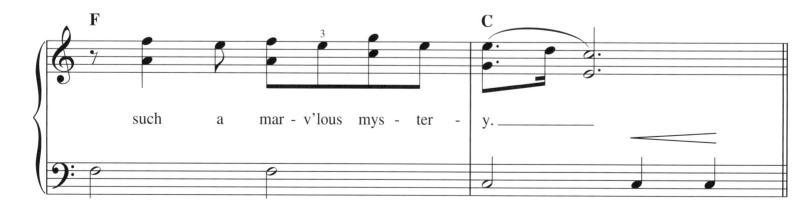

such a mar - v'lous mys - ter - y. _____

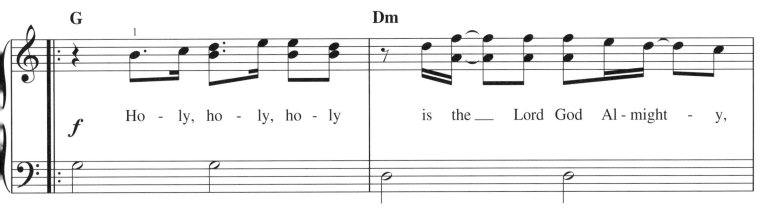

Ho - ly, ho - ly, ho - ly   is the __ Lord God Al - might - y,

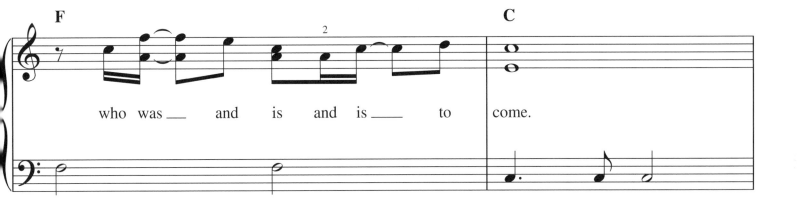

who was __ and is and is ___ to   come.

With all   cre - a - tion, I   sing   praise to   the King of kings. __

1.

You are   my ev - 'ry - thing, __ and   I will ___   a - dore You.

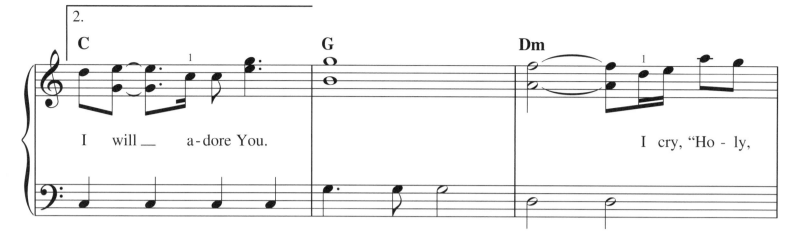

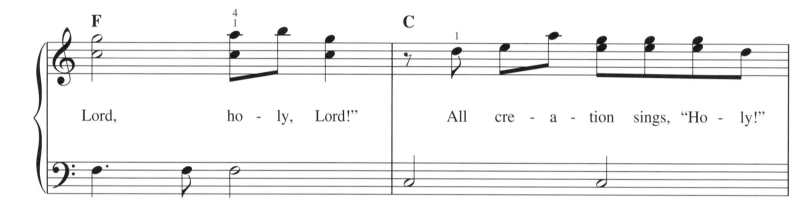

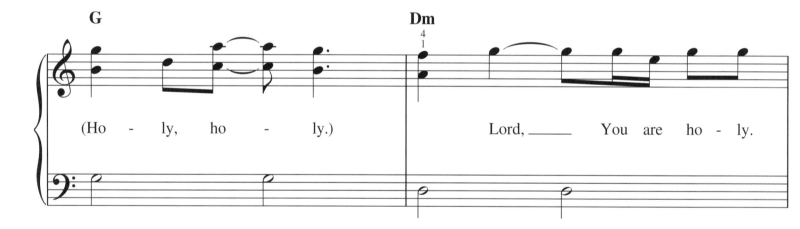

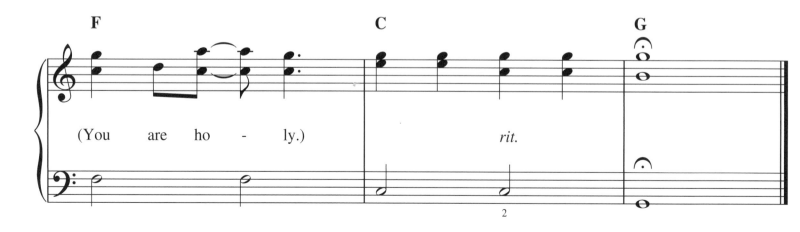